friends

THE SPECIAL QUALITIES OF FRIENDSHIPS
TOLD IN WORDS AND PICTURES BY PAUL FEINBERG

quick fox

THANKS

My thanks to all those who so openly shared part of the experience of a special friendship. My apologies to those whose stories because of time and space limitations could not be included in this volume. Hopefully, there will be a next time.

A special thanks to those generous people whose aid and support contributed in important ways to this book: George Asman, Donna Barker, Art Buchwald, Jim Charlton, Chuck Conconni, Henry Gibson, Richard Gimmaria, Larry L. King, Jack Limpert, Carrie McKee, Joel Siegel, Norma Storch, and Jane Thayer.

And lastly my appreciation and love to Marian Orenstein for her painstaking transcription of all the conversations for this book and for being a terrific sister.

To Anna, Marian, Jane and Joel.

FOREWORD

There are degrees of friendship. The blonde you met on the airplane may have been cordial, indeed, in her time—but likely her time did not last. There is the neighbor with whom you exchange back-fence pleasantries and share an annual drink, but little comes of it. There are the guys from the office and the hardy regulars at the neighborhood quaffery; though you may share some few special moments with them, their names do not pop to mind when it's time to borrow serious money, confess a perfidy, or bury the dead.

Perhaps there is a bit of narcissism in most close friendships. Plain old mirror imagery. Finding much to admire in someone rather like ourselves may be embarrassing, though it's difficult to prove that it constitutes perversion. People just naturally tend to cluster with those who share common interests and outlooks. I mean, who would suggest that Hitler and Helen Keller might have hit it off?

Any *real* friendship requires a long history. The parties to it must have a considerable investment in each other. The best test of a friendship is how well it wears, how it stands up across time. There is nothing quite so disheartening, so likely to breed or sponsor *angst,* as to visit some old former companion and find that—inexplicably— you are in the presence of a stranger wearing a familiar face. Friendships wither if left unattended or if only sporadically hoed out. No amount of "remembering when," looking at old snapshots, or other forms of forced gaiety will bring them back.

True friendships will survive cussing matches, fist fights, and occasional political betrayals. A true friend will understand when the money you owe him is a bit late; more importantly, he will let you have money even when he's a bit short himself and will not require air-tight proof of your need. If in turn he is an *exceptional* friend, he will never, never try to borrow money from you.

A true friend will not make fun of you the day after you've cried in your 3 a.m. beer, or ask what the tears were about. He will cheerfully abandon his midnight comforts to bail you out of jail and will enthusiastically agree when you claim to have been victimized by a miscarriage of justice. Later, at your trial, he will hoot at or ignore that evidence most embarrassing to your cause. He then will lead the way in raising money for your appeal.

A true friend will not mind your interrupting him, even if he's telling a funny story or one tending to heap high honors upon himself. He will voluntarily take the fat girl when, in tandem, you chance upon her and a comely friend. He will lose or gain weight so that his clothes always fit you when needed, and will thoughtfully keep them in good repair. He will take you on trips and never forget your birthday unless you don't want to be reminded of it. He will not become churlish when you fail to meet him at Dallas airport on account of having got off the plane in Omaha to better acquaint yourself with that blonde. He will do blame near anything for you and require nothing in return.

I wish I had such a friend. Unfortunately, I must make do with Warren Burnett. We're stuck with each other and our respective personalities. But, as Lyndon Johnson used to say, "If you can't get the whole loaf, a slice of bread is better than going hungry." —Larry L. King

Washington, D.C., Sept. '80

INTRODUCTION

Most of my life I had no close friendships. It's not that I didn't want to have a pal or a confidant, but I didn't know how to be one, so that right pal just never came along.

My relationships began to change a few years ago after I took up photography. My first magazine assignment, a series of documentary stories on city neighborhoods, enabled me to enter people's private environments. Invariably I kept going back to see the people I had photographed.

At first I thought I was satisfying an old curiosity about people. But it was more than that. I felt a bond to people who had allowed me to photograph them. They let me into their lives and in turn I let them into mine.

As intimacy became easier for me, I didn't need to protect myself from people. I didn't have to be careful anymore. And after a time, I finally found those elusive pals.

What are the possibilities between people who like and trust each other? My new friendships gave me more insight, but I wanted to know more. So I explored the question, first with people I knew and later with strangers I sought out.

This book is a record of what I found. It is also my celebration of having friends, some of whom are included in this book. —Paul Feinberg

friends

LISA ORENSTEIN
Age 5

PETER THOMPSON
Age 5

Lisa: I picked him in nursery school and I picked him because he's handsome and I like his personality and because he wears my favorite colors.

He's nice to me and he doesn't do anything bad except sometimes and that's only a little, and he doesn't cry that much.

When we hear music, we dance by ourselves. We usually play the records that we each want to play. If he doesn't want to play the record that I want to play, we put on half of mine and half of his.

When I come over to his house, he dresses real nice. He does a lot of things that are funny. He makes faces at me.

We read stories to each other. Most of the time we sit next to each other because that's what friends do.

He plays when I want to play, and he plays on things that I want to play sometimes. When you don't have a best friend, there is nobody to play with really.

SERVING GEORGETOWN SINCE 1883
FINEST SELECTION OF...
IMPORTED HAND-MADE
CIGARS INTOWN

ART BUCHWALD
Humorist

HARRY "DOC" DALINSKY
Pharmacist

Buchwald: He taught me everything I know about women.

Dalinsky: He is the worst pupil I ever had.

Buchwald: You have got to have somebody. Whenever I have a problem, I call Doc up, and he has a solution. You tell him things, and he doesn't tell anybody. He's a great man.

If I say that I know Doc, people are impressed. My status usually goes up.

Dalinsky: I told him I can't keep pulling him along any more. Sooner or later he has got to be on his own.

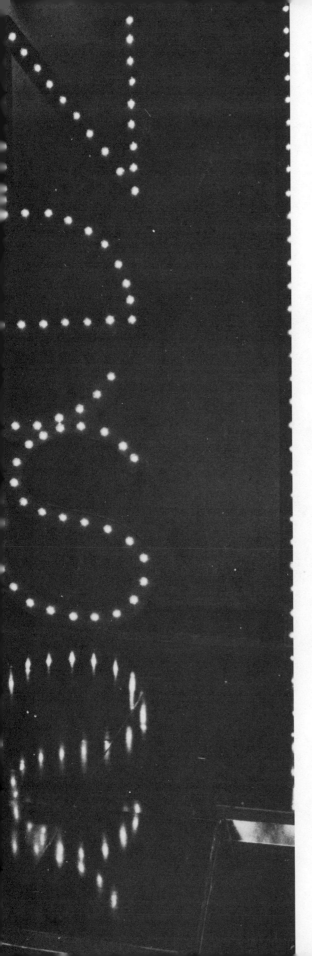

PAT McCORMICK
Comedian

PAUL WILLIAMS
Entertainer

McCormick: It's difficult especially in show business to find someone like Paul who I not only respect and enjoy but can rely on. I appreciate our friendship and try to maintain and nourish it.

He listens to me and does everything I tell him to do because if he doesn't, he knows I'll fall on him.

Williams: I always see a lot of myself in Pat. That's because I can see my reflection in his belt buckle.

LAUREN ORENSTEIN
Age 10

HOLLY THOMPSON
Age 10

Lauren: I can tease Holly, and she won't go and tell the teacher. She doesn't argue too much. She doesn't take everything seriously.

She laughs a lot. When I'm sad, she tries to cheer me up and make me laugh.

She knows everything about me. If I tell her a secret, she doesn't tell, especially if she promised. One night at a slumber party, these girls kept asking Holly to tell about this boy that talked to me. Holly wouldn't tell. Me and Holly stuck together.

We've been friends since nursery school. If I didn't have Holly it seems like I'd be nowhere, just sitting there bored all day. No matter what, we promised each other that we would never not keep in touch—even if I were in Africa.

JAMES BOYD
Hotel porter

ALEXANDER REYNOLDS
Hotel doorman

Reynolds: I say without reservation that James Boyd, normally called Jimmy, is my best friend. He's such an outstanding person of high character and he's very dependable—one whom I can really put my trust in. I've proven that without a shadow of a doubt. James is someone who does things not looking for gain or reward and who I feel will come to my rescue without being asked.

I'll give you an example of how much I think of him: I told my wife a few weeks ago that if I would die unexpectedly she is to go first to James Boyd if she is in any difficulties. He will know what to do, and he will do it. That is a friend.

He knows so much about so many things. He's a person I can ask any advice. He is a reservoir of knowledge and goodness.

MANON CLEARY
Artist

GAY GLADING
Artist

Cleary: Our similarities—we're both artists in a nonart city, both single women in our mid-thirties, ambitious and frightened— give us an insight into each other's feelings and concerns.

There's a strong respect for what can and cannot be violated. We don't step on each other's mental toes. We don't burst each other's bubbles. I don't take criticism well, and Gay doesn't criticize—unless I ask.

There's a certain comfortable predictability with our friendship. I know that if I have a juicy bit of gossip or am in a funny or sad mood, I can always call her up and get some response that is satisfying. She's like having a sister without all the obligations one has to a relative by birth.

Glading: She makes me laugh. I enjoy her teenage locker-room humor and her wonderful stories of her youth that she refuses to forget.

Our friendship is one constant in my life. It's always there, and I can call up and tap it when I need it.

RANDY TAYLOR
Plumber's assistant

ROBERT SULLIVAN
Painter

Taylor: Robert's the only one in his family that hasn't gone to college. He's very intelligent though. His father is very high up; my step-father is a plumber. They have such a good life. I always felt that I really couldn't get along with Robert because his family is so much better than my family.

And at first Robert and myself didn't get along at all. He didn't like me because of where my head was at. I was running around with the wrong kind of people.

After I came out of service, my head was a million miles away from where it was before I went in. We met again and almost everyday we were hanging around. The next thing I know, he's my best friend.

Neither one of us have any enemies. Everyone likes us. The people we don't get along with, that don't mean we don't associate with them. We know where their heads is at, and we know where our head is at.

I'm very open with Robert and I'll tell him anything. If I think his girlfriend looks like a rabbit, I'll tell him. I would never go over Robert's head, and he would never go over my head.

I got very upset when I was away for a couple of weeks and when I came back Robert had this new friend named John. They were acting good buddy-buddy, and Robert wasn't paying that much attention to me.

I figured out where John's head was, but Robert couldn't see it. A few months later John started getting over on Robert and took him for some money. I didn't say anything. I just smiled and Robert realized that the guy got over on him and, like, apologized to me.

We see John now, and Robert and I smile and just shake our heads. John don't know where our head is at.

MULUMEBET BEKELE

YONAS BIRU
Student

LINDA FREES
Airline agent

Frees: I first heard about Mulumebet
through Yonas, who works at the same
hotel where I moonlight. Most hotels have
their own foreign contingents because
hotel jobs don't pay much, and only
poorer people or foreigners take them.
He's the bellman on the shift I'm on. In
slack periods we started talking and became friends.

Yonas escaped Ethiopia about a year ago.
He differed politically from the govern-
ment. They killed his father. He went
through hell getting out of the country.
Mulumebet helped Yonas escape. She
kept him alive and went to prison for it.

He'd been trying to get Mulumebet to
America. As a last resort he asked me to
help him and to sign the support affidavit
that I would be responsible for her. That's
normally the kind of thing I shy away
from but somebody has to be there when
you need help. We can't go through our
busy, isolated lives without reaching out
and giving something of ourselves.

Mulumebet finally arrived yesterday.
Yonas has been so excited. I'm so happy
for him. He's made me feel so much
better about what America is all about.

"IKE" FREEMAN
Physician

TOD DUNCAN
Opera singer

Duncan: We were five old fishing buddies.
They were precious and dear friends. Dr.
Freeman and I are the only two left. For
forty years the sea has tied us together.

There's nothing that Ike Freeman and I
haven't straight-eyed discussed in a fishing
boat. We follow the whole watershed of
life, we confront its so-called problems,
we talk philosophy. I never left being with
Ike Freeman that I didn't feel a better
man.

There's something about sharing the sea
with a person that makes for a deeper
comradery. We're more real out there.
There's no perfunctory artificial stuff,
no cosmetic stuff. You either catch a fish
or you don't.

MICHAEL HAUPTSCHEIN
Photographer

SHELDON LITT
Gestalt therapist

Hauptschein: In high school he was the intellectual, but he didn't know how to dress right or talk to girls, so I taught him. We parted for a while, but after all our friends got married we had a rebirth of our friendship.

When he comes here, we look up old friends. That usually makes us feel good that we didn't get married. He still has a crush on his junior high school girlfriend. He looks at that same picture of her every year and reminisces how it could have been if her mother hadn't kicked him out of the house.

He's a character. Even people that don't like him find him interesting. He took me to this big encounter group because he thought it would be a good place to pick up girls. At the end of the session, our group voted me most likable because of my eyes and voted Sheldon least likable. The encounter leader wanted Sheldon to come on stage to find out why no one liked him and said, "Will Shelby please come on stage?"

Sheldon hollered out, "It's not Shelby. It's Sheldon." It just so happens the guy Sheldon hates most in the world is named Shelby.

The leader again asked, "Will Shelby come on stage?" Even louder Sheldon screamed, "It's Sheldon, not Shelby and I'm not coming on stage."

The next day Sheldon was still a little upset, and when we ran into a shrink friend of his, Sheldon asked him to look into my eyes to see what about my eyes had made me so likable. The shrink stared into my eyes and then turned to Sheldon and said, "They look vacant to me."

That made Sheldon feel better.

Litt: When I get fed up with New York, I come down to Washington and stay with Michael so I can relax and escape to peace and quiet. We hang out together. He fixes me up with girls. We sit around and talk about the old days and all the schmucks who got married.

He's the only person who writes me. I like to keep in touch, I need to check in. I need someone to complain to who sees the world the same way as I do in terms of frustrations and disappointments.

ADMIRAL ROBERT MORRIS
United States Navy officer, retired

PEGGY LOAR
Assistant director of cultural institute

Morris: For God's reasons, to serve his purpose, he must have said, "Well, Bobby, I've got just so much time for you around here, and I've got a job for you to do, and when you need a rainbow in the sky, I'll bring it." Peggy was that rainbow.

Loar: I don't look upon him as a father-or grandfather-figure in spite of his age. He's the most unusual friend I've ever had. I find him warm, witty, brilliant, and sometimes crazy.

He is fresh air in a world that for me is very complicated and hard-driving and restless. The creek by his house is calm, and he exudes that calmness for me. I'm so delighted to be able to share something that is so important to him, which is his space and quiet life.

I find myself searching for ways to please him, special things to do for him, but he makes it so clear that being present is all that I need to do.

KERSTIN POLLACK
Executive, science foundation

REGINALD POLLACK
Artist

Kerstin: He's yummy. He cheers up my life. Without him there wouldn't be any joy. There would be no reason for doing anything. I would not exist.

CHRISTENE DUNN
Age 15

ANGEL FLYNN
Age 15

Dunn: To a lot of people, a person is like a shell. They just look on the outside and judge only by outer appearances.

When I look at Angel, I don't see her physical features. I see mostly the person inside, which is a person like me. She feels a lot of things that she doesn't understand, but tries to understand. She wants to be real to someone and wants to share with someone the things in life that touch her.

LOW MOAN
SPECTACULAR

Comedy group

Left to right: Joe Perotte, Mark Blank-
field, Brandes Kemp, Diz White, Ron House,
Mitch Krundel, Allan Shearman.

We're like kids playing together. It's a most
wonderful concept.

SUGAR RAY LEONARD
Boxer

JOE BROADY
Security guard

Leonard: A couple of guys were boxing in the backyard. I saw Joe was dominating and outclassing these guys. I was then just in the early stages of my career in the amateurs. I put the gloves on with Joe and hit him so hard he said, "Somebody turned the lights out." Ever since then we've been swinging together and boxing together.

Now I pretty much can buy or have anything I want. But I need someone to help me keep my head on right, someone I can talk to outside the ring, someone I can kid with, someone I can pound on when I have to.

He was there before I had anything. Joe will always be there.

Broady: I out-pointed everybody that was boxing in Palmer Park. One day this guy they called "Ray Charles," who lives in the court, comes around, and we boxed a couple of rounds. He was smaller then, but gee-whiz his left hook stayed. He had the talent.

We competed in tournaments together. I won the Golden Gloves in '73. He went on to the Olympics. We used to sit back and just fantasize about winning a title and big cars and fancy clothes and lots of money.

It's behind me now. One of us made it and one of us didn't. He had the will power and determination to stick it out. If I had stayed in the gym and pushed it like him, I might have made it too. But I guess everybody has a sad story.

STEVE WYSOCKI
Student

CHARLIE WYSOCKI
University student and football star

Steve: We played football together in high school. I got along real good with him so I invited him over to the house a couple of times. Then he started coming over on his own, even when I wasn't home. He would talk to my mom and dad. You could see he needed someone to tell his problems to. All this love started pouring out of him and that started bringing us closer together as a family.

He wanted to move in with us. We wanted him to stay because we loved him, and he needed us. We waited a few months till we were all sure, and we went through with the proceedures and adopted him. Now he's ours, and no one can take him away from us, and I've got the big brother I always wanted.

Charlie: Where I used to live, if something happened, no matter what, they'd say, "You did it. You were the one who did it." "I didn't do it." "No. You did it," and I got beaten for that. "Trust me," I said, but no one trusted me, and I always heard I was going to be a bum.

My new family gives me the courage and support I need. If I am up, they are up. If I am down, they are up and try to keep me up. They never condemn me for doing anything wrong.

My family is my closest friend. There's a lot of lost time I have to make up. I don't need anyone else as long as I have my self-esteem and my family backing me up.

LARRY KING
Author/playwright

WARREN EDSEL BURNETT
Lawyer

King: Our personalities are so goddamn churlish most folks won't put up with the degree of bullshit that we both hand out, so each of us had to find somebody to be tolerant of the other. Burnett was the first politician I ran into with a sense of humor and a sense of the absurd, and he also would get drunk with me before noon and go on the radio station and say anything I wanted him to or talk about subjects calculated to get him into trouble.

He was running for district attorney for Hector and Midland counties in west Texas. I had the twelve noon news show on radio station KCRS. He was then unmarried, twenty-four, he claimed twenty-three, but looked eighteen.

Burnett was running against an old man, Charlie Butts, who was thirty-one and had three or four children. Butts was running ads in the paper which showed his family and by implication was saying Burnett was a young fellow chasing women and going out drinking too much.

We fell to drinking at 10:30 in the morning. By my noon show, we were pretty drunk. Burnett invented himself by going on the air over a two-county-wide hookup and announcing that the campaign had boiled down to one of "ability versus virility" which became the number one slogan politically out there for the rest of the year. Much to his astonishment and mine, he carried both counties and won the race.

Burnett: We just never disagree on our enemies and talk very little about our friends. We unite in great hate against community leaders, preachers, most Texas politicians, bankers—everything that's puffed.

We don't talk about our likes. There's just never been time; there's so much damn hate to be articulated.

ARNY LIPIN
ARNIE CARR

Carr: I was in a pretty isolated space when I was ill with Hodgkin's disease. It's hard to talk to people about what you're experiencing because their fears get in the way. It's hard to talk about death, chemotheraphy, or lots of private things because they all want you to get better and are rooting for you, but they try to deny your struggle in dying.

So I went to this holistic health center where many people who are struggling with all sorts of threatening illnesses go. There I felt a great sense of support and acceptance. It was a sanctuary, an oasis.

I met Arny at the center. He has Gehrig's disease, a muscular degeneration. We share a lot of letting go of the same things—of ego and ambition. When I first met him, he was walking with crutches. He could drive. He was still seeking a cure. The more he lost his physical powers and his body fell away, the more his heart seemed to open.

Lipin: I lived most of my life without allowing people to get close to me. When I became ill, many things started changing for me besides what was going on in my body. I was no longer competing with anyone. Success was no longer a criterion for worth. That allowed me to have a vulnerability, and I became a more genuine and loving person.

Most of my friendships before had been based exclusively on doing things. There was a couple that we'd go dancing with, or a movie couple, or a travel couple. These relationships never got beyond the superficial.

I never let any of them in because deep down I was afraid that what they might discover about me was unworthy. I found out it was all in my head. It wasn't anything unworthy at all. It was only my unfulfilled expectations, my judgments of myself. My "critic" was going crazy and I was listening to him. I still hear him when he speaks, but I no longer listen to him.

There's nothing unspoken now. Arnie and I show ourselves to be scared. We embrace each other and give open affection to each other. There are no judgments or expectations. It's all O.K. It's today and not a ten-year investment.

RANDY ZEIBERT
Restaurant manager

DUKE ZEIBERT
Restaurant owner

Duke: I have thousands of friends, but I think of my son as my best friend. It only got that way in the last couple of years. I changed, became wiser, and he grew up. I had to wait till he lost that little-boy naiveness.

He is young and patient and level-headed—a college graduate. I am old and impatient. I'm an old alley cat who came up the hard way, scratching—from the school of hard knocks.

Now we understand and respect each other. We enjoy each other's company. We go out together. When one of us asks the other for money, we give it without questioning. If you can put your hand in a friend's pocket and he can put his hand in your pocket, and you don't bat an eyelash either way, that is the highest form of friendship you can have, and I have that with my son.

SVETLANA GODILLA

Astrologer

Godilla: In the past I have had to flee from one country to another. So if you have no possessions, no money, and no family, you'd better hold on to your friends. And if you have problems you cannot always burden one person. So it certainly does help if you have more close friends than one, and I've got seven best friends.

My friends have two common denominators—intelligence and heart. Each is young in spirit whether they're thirty or sixty years old. All want to learn; their span of interest is tremendous. They are pliable, flexible, courageous, and creative and have a good sense of humor and can laugh about themselves.

With my best friends we share with one another either good or bad. We hold each other's hands when it's necessary, and we dance with one another when it's necessary.

JOHN J. SIRICA
Judge

MILTON S. KRONHEIM
Liquor distributor

Sirica: You meet a lot of phony people in your life, but he's an honest, down-to-earth person who's never forgotten his rough-and-tumble days, when he was coming up like myself. My instincts tell me he's sincere in his feelings toward me, and he has my interests at heart.

I don't know of any man that's more loved by more people—that's a pretty good recommendation. He treats a broken-down bum or a kid with respect. That's what I call a real man.

Kronheim: When we were young, we'd go to the gym and box or play handball or clown around together. I was no match for him when we boxed. I was bigger than him, but that didn't mean a thing. He could have killed me any time he wanted to, but he was very charitable to me with the gloves; except the time I got a little fresh, and he hit me one extra little tap and gave me a black eye to put me in my place.

We like each other. There are no ulterior motives. So we've maintained our friendship over the years, always enjoying each other's company but never expecting too much from each other. Gratitude is a small virtue, but ingratitude can become a large vice.

SID SUSSMAN
Beauty pageant director

DEBBIE SHELTON
TV actress

Sussman: I've conducted 1,800 beauty pageants and had more national winners than anybody who ever lived. What is America anyway—bread and butter, apple pie, and girls. The minute they do away with girls, you don't need magazines, you don't need bars, you don't need anything. When you stop looking at girls, the party's over.

To me it's fun to take some yoyo who's got potential, break her head open, fill it up with the right kind of stuff, and see her six months later go and rule the world. I sit back and know I was part of it. I helped create it.

So there is a great tendency for a beautiful girl to get into a relationship with me because of what I can or might do for her. She appreciates the fact that I might make her a star, introducing her to celebrities or taking her to important parties or getting her picture in magazines. In a round-about way, I'm actually buying the girl. But I never feel that I can afford buying a girl because there is always someone who can come along that can outbuy me.

"Gimme, gimme, gimme." Sometimes I was easy, and I did. And then it becomes a matter of pride; you don't want to be embarrassed, or made a fool of.

So they went their directions, I went mine. Occasionally, I see them in movies or on TV, but I don't really hear from any of them except one—Debbie Shelton. She played the game pretty straight with me.

It's been more than ten years since she won the title. She's a superstar now. But out of the clear blue she'll still show up on my doorstep and say, "Let's eat." Or I'll get this package in the mail and it's a chocolate Easter egg. That's the way she is—warm, exciting, and fun. Even today I still use her as a measurement of how good you can be in this business.

BARRY GOLDWATER, SR.
United States senator

GENERAL WILLIAM QUINN
United States Army officer, retired

Goldwater: He was Army and I was Air Force. So we started right off fighting, and we never quit. He chews my ass out if he doesn't like what I do. He's always given me straight answers.

I get to my office about 7:30 A.M. each day. I have a stack of mail a foot high. I have to stay in the office all day and have to see a lot of people, some of whom, with their bitches and gripes, I really don't enjoy seeing.

So when Fridays come, I can't wait to get to Bill's farm on the eastern shore where we spend the weekends together and where it's next to impossible to be found. We put on our old clothes and don't give a damn how we look or what we say.

He'll have a different list ready each weekend marked "Goldy." I know that I'm supposed to do everything on that list— like repair the toilet, fix the light circuits, cut the wood, or make the tractor run; I do the mechanical and electrical work, which I enjoy, and he takes care of the esoteric. We make a great team.

Westerners are not prolific in their search for friends, but I daresay nobody in this world can name more real friends than he has five fingers. And when you find a real friend like Bill, by God, you've got a friend.

Quinn: He puts up with me, and I'm a lousy character and know it. He can accept that, so he's got to be a very special friend.

"CAPTAIN BILLY" TINDELL
Retired

TAYLOR BURKE
Bank president

Burke: I went to a party one night, and there was this guy in the corner with his back to everyone, sitting by himself, looking into the corner. I said, "Who's that?" and they said, "That's James Tindell, and he doesn't like anybody."

I thought that sounds like an interesting person worth meeting. So I went back in the corner, pulled up a chair and said, "Do you mind if I join you?" He said, "I certainly do mind, shove off." We've been friends ever since.

He's a rather bad person. He sees what he should not see, and he doesn't see what he should see. There's no health in it. It takes six drinks to get him up to par, to where he can walk and talk and smile at people and drive cars and operate machinery.

Nobody likes him but me. I'm the only person in town who will talk to him. Everybody has to have one friend, the burdens we take on, and mine is being a friend to Captain Billy.

Tindell: It's very irritating for two old men like us, who just want to sip and mind our own business, and now our sons keep bringing around their nubile Greek women with not a straight line anywhere on them. We started wearing dark glasses and don't look too much and drink a lot and hope "it" will go away. It's the saddest thing that can happen to man: when the sexual revolution got here, we're out of ammunition. We fired our last artillery twenty years ago.

Colonel and I had a vasectomy a few years ago. We went together; we got good rates. We were both a little afraid so we held hands.

They said it wouldn't but it hurt like hell. It feels like you've been kicked and you walk a little funny. People will ask, "What's the matter with you?" Say "stomach ache;" you don't want to tell them.

We had been told by women at the bridge club that men who have had vasectomys suddenly develop a certain devil-may-care attitude and perform beautifully. We had never performed very well even in our best days. So we decided that we would develop this rakish attitude and assault young women and leave no traces behind us.

But it took us six months before it stopped hurting enough to think about anything like that. Now we take our little certificates out to show to girls, but it doesn't seem to have the desired effect; they look at you like you were a steer or something.

Burke: But since Captain had his vasectomy, there seems to be less big-eared children running around town.

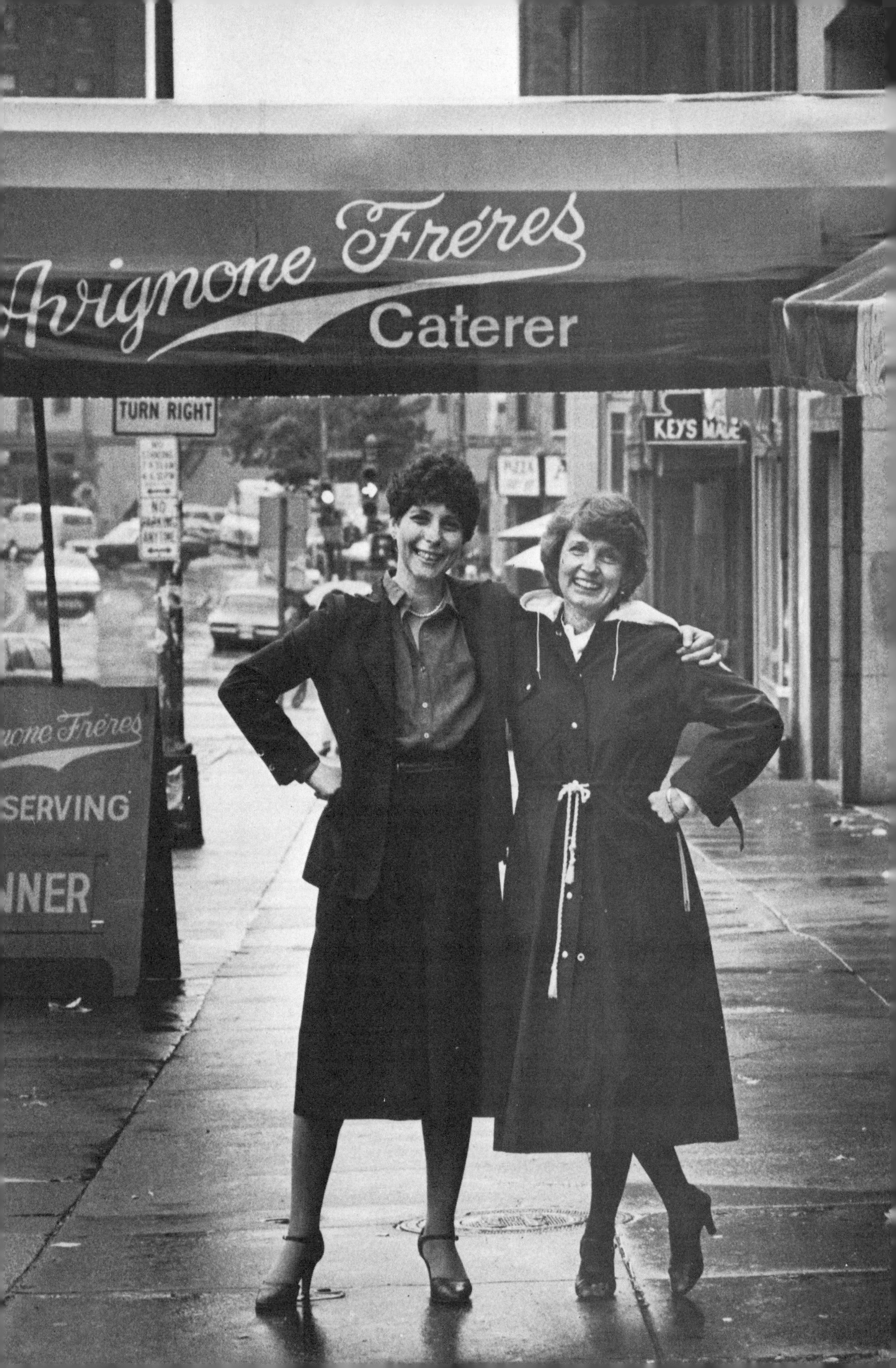
Avignone Fréres
Caterer
TURN RIGHT
KEYS MADE
SERVING
NNER

GRACE CAVELIERI
Poet/playwright/TV executive

JANET HINES GUNZENHAUSER
Treasurer, manufacturing company

Cavelieri: I bring her joy. She shows it. She appreciates me. There's nothing I say that bores her. I'm fully realized. I can't believe my luck.

She was the most outstanding student at Trenton High and the most beautiful and the most loved. I idolized her.

I'm haunted by the past, its like being close to your dream world. Since my parents are dead, Jan is the only one that knows how it felt. She owns a little piece of my life. It comes from knowing each other when we were babies, growing up on the same block, going to mass and the same schools together. Everything we felt walking from school together, we'll feel when we're seventy-five. We're going to be old together.

Gunzenhauser: I'm not a leader. I go along with things. There have to be followers in this world. I can build on things, but I don't have the guts to do a lot of things by myself. But I do when Gracie says let's do it. Gracie does all the courageous things.

Being of our background and the times we grew up in, you got married, did all the expected things and were happy like in *Father Knows Best*. Gracie was my safety valve. If I bitched or complained to her, I didn't feel I was doing the wrong thing. And when I didn't feel loved, it didn't matter that my mother cared; I needed soothing from Gracie.

I told my husband before he met Gracie, I remember it clearly, the first stand I ever took. "You're going to meet my best friend and you must like her and you must accept her because this is the one person I will not give up."

PATT LINTON
Age 13

SUSIE BORKENHAGEN
Age 12

We're so wild. We're game to do anything. We always act crazy and get in trouble no matter where we go. In school Mr. Hennessey can't stand us cause we bug people and are so bad. It's hard to find people like us.

JERRY HANSON
Department store buyer

PRISCILLA AYCOCK
Budget analyst

Aycock: In the beginning, I had Jerry up on a pedestal. I wanted to be like her. I thought that if I could look like her and had ideas and enjoyed the same things, my life would be better.

Then one day, I realized that that was stupid. I couldn't be someone else, and I didn't have to be Jerry for her to approve of me. So now I'm just me, and she likes just me.

Jerry motivates me. I'm very sedentary. I think I could sit in a room reading a book for the rest of my life if someone didn't give me a push now and then.

When Jerry comes around, I feel like getting up and doing things and seeing what's out there. I'm up and energetic for a long time afterward—like I've had my battery recharged.

GENERAL HOWARD C. DAVIDSON

United States Army officer, retired

ADMIRAL RAYMOND P. HUNTER

United States Army officer, retired

Hunter: The general, even at ninety, has the most amazing memory of anyone I've ever known. I'm forever learning new and wonderful things about life from the stories he tells. He quotes songs, poetry, books and even people he served with on the Mexican border in 1913—when he was chasing Pancho Villa.

He's always taking classes or learning something new. It's hard keeping up with him, but I enjoy trying.

Davidson: I'm West Point, class of 1913; he's Annapolis, class of 1931. My class was dying out so our two classes have had joint meetings for years. We're supposed to hate the hell out of each other, but it didn't work out that way; if we do, we certainly backslide.

We make things together. We don't have the foggiest idea why, but it's more fun to do it together. Ray retired in 1959 and started coming over here, now he comes over almost every day. We don't have a punishing schedule of applying ourselves to any task at hand. We work till noon, knock off and drink some sherry, and have a lunch and excellent conversation. Then I lie down, and Ray stays and finishes up.

I don't think we thought we were friends. As Pericles said, we are "woven into the stuff of other men's lives." I don't know how we got woven or why, but it really doesn't matter.

DAVID LANCE GOINES
Lithographer

ALICE WATERS
Restaurant owner and chef

Goines: We had been lovers years ago. Now we're just friends but in a way that isn't present between people who haven't had sexual intimacy. Deep fears and alienness are dissolved after a period of time, and you reveal yourself in ways that you can't share even with your closest friends.

I don't think the lover part of our relationship went away; it's just not being kept up, and there's been a long gap that's probably going to last the rest of our lives.

I'd probably die without our friendship. It's like a diet of good, high-quality food where I've ended up healthy and mentally stable as a result.

You need certain things in order to live. What kills people is loneliness and not being valuable to anybody.

LOIS GIBSON
HENRY GIBSON

Henry: Not only is there a wife whom I love and share with, but there is this extra added bonus of someone I want to be with more than anyone else. It's either a sign of my desperation that there's no one else, or it's an unusual, right, lucky coming together. All of our friends hate us because we don't have time for anybody except each other.

Before Lois, I was potential. Afterwards I became whole, full, and real.

Lois: The first night I met him he quoted half of Homer in Greek. I thought he was the cutest thing I'd ever seen in my life, but couldn't understand what we had in common except liking each other. He moved in that evening and has never left.

I get great gratification from being with Henry. When we are together, our creativity is one another.

I always feel incomplete without him.

Henry: I always feel incomplete without you.

Lois: Well, I didn't know that! I thought I was the one getting completed.

JAMES BRAGG
Jail classification and parole officer

BILLY NEAL
Jail inmate

Neal: I've been around the system for twenty-three years. I've come in and out eight or nine times. I kept messing up. It's the same soup but different ingredients.

He gave me confidence in myself. Nobody had never accepted me. He gives me something, but he don't look for anything in return. He's down to earth. He don't stroke it. He's not jiving. He wants to see me do all right.

For the first time in my life I'm conscious of my age. I'm not young any more, and I want my freedom. I want to enjoy what other people enjoy, to take care of my family myself, to be a man once in life.

Bragg: There's so much turmoil and so little love. People just don't care about one another. There's a thin line between his background and mine. But somebody helped me as a kid; nobody helped Billy.

I care about Billy. I like him as a person. I think he has the basic qualities to succeed in the streets. I think he now has what he didn't have before—people that believe in him. I know he can make it.

BETTY ROGOWSKY
Cafeteria assistant

PATTY POWELL
Cafeteria assistant

Rogowsky: We gossip behind the counter. She talks a lot about her customers. She flirts with her favorites. She's outspoken. She tells me when a customer has a nice ass or walks just right. She makes me blush a lot. She can communicate with guys much better than I can.

Powell: But she's the one with a fiancé. She's finally doing it before I do it and I'm going to cry on the wedding day.

But I want her to think more about getting married, since this is her first real boy friend and it seems like her and Scott are always fighting about something stupid.

She never has any money now. She pays for all his things. A man should pay for his own school, gas and food. Why should I spend my hard earned money on a guy? He should get a job and spend his money on me.

Rogowsky: If she was in love, she'd feel a little different. When he gets out of school and gets a job, she'll be more at ease. That's why he's going to school: to get a good job so we can live happy and not poor.

She's been through a lot more than I have. I don't mind her being concerned. She just wants me to be sure.

JOHN LABERT
Retired, Old Soldiers Home

CHRISTOPHER "OBIE" O'BRIEN
Retired, Old Soldiers Home

O'Brien: I was drafted in '42. I was forty years old. Them days they were grabbing anybody; all they wanted was a body. I came to the Home in '67 after I had a cancer operation. I'm living thirteen years on borrowed time.

I come to this bar every day 'cause it's close to the Home, and I have a drink. One year at Christmas, John, he's a sociable kind of guy, came to my table and wished me a Merry Christmas—and that's how we first got acquainted.

So after that we got to talking. He's been places I've been, and we talk about it. He's a nice, pleasant guy and tells me about his family and this and that, and he brings in the news every day.

Labert: He came in the bar one day, a little short guy with a black coat. I told him he looked like an undertaker. That just tickled the hell out of me and him, and I invited him to have a C&C with me. Now we sit together when we're here. He's someone to talk to and pass away the time with.

CATHAY BOMAR
Student

ALEXANDRA TRUITT
Student

Bomar: I'd go bonkers if I didn't have Alex because people like myself don't get along with too many people. I don't seem to fit into this WASPISH world that I want to fit into. I have this image of myself that if some young man brought me home, his mother would clutch at her heart at seeing this whorish-looking half-breed.

Alex is the personification of all that's respectable—the ultimate WASP with blond hair and blue eyes. The fact that she could accept me for what I am never ceases to amaze me.

She legitimized my presence. She makes me feel totally secure and like I belong. When I'm on her arm, I feel safe and strong.

JOHN McEVOY
Retired

JESSE H. HUEY
Retired

Mr. McEvoy says he has never in his life allowed his picture to be taken and is "not going to start now."

McEvoy: We don't go any place. We don't do anything. We read a lot. We drink a little beer once in a while. We find out things about each other that the police haven't found out yet. We philosophize about everything. I respect his opinions, and he respects mine to a certain extent. We get along just like two he-bears—peaceable, more or less.

Huey: I don't want to be his friend; I'm just stuck with him.

He tells a few lies once in a while, but I like him and I like to hear his lies. The Irish lie a lot, you know. In the fantasy land he lives in, in all that senility, he thinks I believe him.

But he's a gentleman. One of nature's noblemen.

SAM SHANKER
Night club owner

BLAZE STARR
Burlesque stripper

Starr: My first job on the road was for Sam. He's the only one I work for without a contract. It's just like coming home.

He's not greedy. He has consideration for people's feelings. He never told me how much to take off. He don't play with me or any of the girls and he never did even when he was younger. Sam is a gentleman.

Shanker: She's one of the finest troupers in show business. This is a lady. She always behaves herself. Her word means everything.

I've been in this business close to forty years. Show business ain't just what it is any more. These newcomers give me nothing but a headache.

Blaze knows you go out and do a show to the best of her knowledge and gives the public everything she's got.

She makes up right, wears the flashy gowns, gives entertainment: She's what show business is. She's one of the all-timers.

WILLIAM BARLOW
Musicologist

SUNNYLAND SLIM
Blues musician

Sunnyland: Bill and me are poor man's friends. We're scuffling in a way. It's a call and a hello and a how you doing.

I cook soul food, Bill cooks gumbo. We have a good time, he satisfies me.

He gets me jobs where I'm at. If I got a dollar and he needs it, he gets it. Church people don't have that kind of relationship. Everybody wants to go to heaven, but they don't want to sing, pray, or die.

LOUIS KEITH
Professor of medicine

DONALD KEITH
Engineer

Donald: He gives me a sense of calm. I
need him, but it's more than an intellectual
or emotional need. We share the same soul.

NORMAN TAMARKIN
Psychiatrist

JACK WARDEN
Actor

Tamarkin: The work that I do is very demanding. People want a lot from me emotionally and part of my job is to give that in a variety of ways. When I'm not working I don't want someone around whose ego is real fragile. I don't want people who are dependent on my feelings about them, or what I do for them, for their own self-esteem.

He's got a lot going for him. He's very successful. He doesn't need me at all. He likes me and finds me interesting, which is more flattering than being needed.

BARBARA BENEZRA FREEDMAN
Homemaker

ANN GROER
Newspaper correspondent

Groer: She was once a crazy, single lady like me, and we did a lot of watershed things together. In the 1960s we went to California—two fairly cloistered surburbanites in Berkeley, where our friends are doing drugs, going to nude beaches, camping out in Big Sur. It was like sending us to China.

She got married, had two kids and lives in the suburbs, while I live in the ghetto, have a career, and have never been married. Every now and then we look at each other's lives and think "Do we want to change? Trade?"

I'm usually trying to liberate her from motherhood by getting her out of the house and making her do new things. She tries to show me another reality of life that I haven't experienced.

She wants me to get married. There are times when she sounds like she ought to be my mother, and I want to smack her. But there are other times when I run to her for mothering.

Barbara's having two wonderful children has taken the heat off me to have children of my own. It would be nice to have kids, but I'm thirty-four, very single at the moment, and it doesn't look like a prospect. So Barbara's kids are my proxy children.

We made a decision a long time ago that we would be best friends; so we are, and we work at it like people work at marriage.

MARY SWIFT
Writer

HUNTINGTON T. BLOCK
Insurance company president

Swift: He seems the same person that I knew back in our teens. Since he's from the same background and knows how I operate, things don't become overly complicated. There are times when you desperately need people like Bucky who have strong character, set a long time ago, that you can go to for understanding. You know that he'll give you the very best advice.

Block: There's a youth cult in today's world and most relationships are so temporary. But when you have an old friend, like Mary, that you've come a long way with, then you don't mind growing old so much.

The older I get, the more the friendship means. When you are young, you really don't need much, because you've a lot of life ahead of you. When you get older you know you have only so much time left, and you know that you want to have the very most you can get out of that time.

MIKE SEEGER
Folk music performer

ELIZABETH COTTON
Folk music performer

Seeger: She had been doing daywork most of her life when she came to work for our family in the early fifties. It wasn't until four or five years later that we accidentally discovered that Elizabeth could play the guitar.

My sister brought me into the kitchen where Elizabeth played "In the Sweet By and By," first in the church style, Methodist time, and then without missing a beat, she proceeded to rag it—to syncopate. It was the closest I've come to a religious experience. We never knew she could play. I couldn't believe how good she was.

She taught me her style of music, and she shared with me her ways of seeing life. She's very generous and wise and a regal person.

We both started playing professionally about twenty years ago, but she was starting out at age sixty-five, when most people think about retirement. She's still going strong now at a very young eighty-seven; she's amazing.

Cotton: Mike's from a family of people where I never did feel I wasn't welcome. When I worked for them they never treated me like a maid. They treated me like Mrs. Seeger—like family.

Michael's father always said, "We didn't adopt Elizabeth, Elizabeth adopted us."

They were nice children. They were obedient. They never talked back to me. I came to love them so very much.

That love that I had back then is still with me. My feelings for Mike get more and more. The more I'm with him the more I love him.

ABE POLLIN
Owner of professional sports teams

ARNOLD SEIGEL
Professor

Pollin: He's straight, moral, honest, and decent to a point of almost naiveté since he believes that almost everyone in the world is as decent as he is.

Seigel: Reminiscing is the best part of growing old. Abe and I had over forty years of growing up together so we share many pleasant and important memories which allow us to keep the past alive. After forty years we don't have to ask why any more.

ALI-REZA FASHIHI
Dental technician

GUITY MATIN
Couturiere

Matin: I don't act differently or set separate standards for him because he's my son. I don't feel he's an extension of me because I've had him in my body for nine months.

I treat him like other human beings I like or love. We're friends, and if you want to invest in a friendship, who's going to be better than your own son?

I'm completely open with him. I approve of my own behavior, and since I do, there is no reason to hide anything from him. If I come out of the shower and Ali walks in, I don't feel embarrassed and cover myself. Why should I? Who is closer to me than Ali?

Fashihi: She taught me how to live with her and how to live without her. She would say, "You do it yourself. You make your own decisions. I'm not here to make decisions for you."

She lives her life and doesn't depend on me to make her happy. But I know she likes me, and when she worries about me, I know it's out of caring, not obligation.

BOBBY LONG
Member, Phantoms Motorcycle Club

BUTCH MEYERS
Construction worker

Long: The Phantoms are like brothers to me. It's like one big family. It's just like how much you love your mother, that's how much you love the club.

Butch is a citizen; he's not in the club or nothing, but I think as much of him as I do my own brothers in the club.

If I get into a fight, my brothers will help me out; if Butch gets in a fight, I'll help him out. Even if he's wrong, I'll get into it because I don't want to see anyone jump on him.

We've been through a lot together—fighting, drinking, women. Things that I needed, if he'd had it, he'd give it to me. Same thing if he needed something, I'd give it to him.

Meyers: I can trust him. I can leave him with my old lady and she could be laying there naked, and he wouldn't mess with her because he's got respect for me and that's the same way I am with him.

JOHN STEPHENS
Musician

MARGO ST. JAMES
Activist for prostitutes' rights

Stephens: Margo always knows just how far to trust me. She doesn't expect too much from me so she doesn't make demands.

And no matter where she's been living since I've known her, her couch has always been reserved for me. For an itinerant musician, there is nothing more important than a place to rest that you know is always there.

St. James: We're both paupers and don't intend to own anything in our lifetime. We just want enough money so we can eat and a place to live where it's warm and dry.

If someone has run out on me and left me high and dry and broke my heart and stolen all my money or my dope stash, John's shoulder will be there for me to cry on. Then he'll show me a way to laugh about it because he believes a laugh is worth more than anything.

ZACHARIAH D. BLACKISTONE

108 years of age/retired
founder of florist shops

As a little boy I had a bosom friend named
Tom Neal. He was black; his father had
been a slave on our farm. I loved Tom and
he loved me. We used to play together all
the time. He was a good scout, a good boy,
and he liked the things I liked. We liked
them together.

On high tides we would go down to the
mouth of the stream that flowed through
our farm and fish for little minnows. We'd
catch them like nobody's business, but we
never ate them; we'd throw them back in.
That was our play. A lot of fun, a lot of
fun to catch those minnows.

When Tom was older, he went to work for
my uncle, Dr. Pitney Blackistone. He con-
tracted some disease and died when he
wasn't much more than twenty years old.

All my friends are gone now. I can't
remember any of the others except for
Tom Neal. He's the only one I'm able to
remember.

DOUGLAS HARTMAN

Waterproofer

I painted the car like this so people will know I'm different. The scenes painted on it have no significance. Two tombstones are painted on the back. One is for me and one for my buddy who helped me dream up the car. How many people are going to put tombstones on the back of their car? The paint I used is special; it's Rustoleum. As far as I know, nobody has ever tried it for cars.

I just love the car. It's a piece for me. It's like a girlfriend, but it never gives me no back lip. It treats me right, and I treat it right. If it wants something, I give it to it, and it gives me what I want—enjoyment, pleasure.

JACKIE CAIN AND ROY KRAL

Jazz musicians

JOEL E. SIEGEL

University professor/music & film critic

Siegel: I heard my first Jackie and Roy record when I was a teenager at summer camp. Something in their music immediately appealed to me—its sunniness, I suppose, and its precision. I went out and bought all of their albums.

Eight years later, I met them when they were appearing at the Village Vanguard. Although I was shy, we hit it off right away. Afterwards, I don't think I ever got an answer, but I'd see them perform every couple of years, and they'd say that they liked hearing from me. It was a very abstract relationship. I guess they represented creativity and beauty for me, things that were missing from my life then.

A few years ago, I interviewed them for a jazz magazine and we became very close. The age difference, a bit too wide when I was younger, seemed to have narrowed. In fact, they now looked younger than I did, which wasn't quite fair. As we talked we discovered that we were both facing the deaths by cancer of persons very dear to us. They were most understanding and supportive, which helped me through some bad times.

These days, we hang out together and do what friends do—swap visits, songs, secrets, books, jokes, gossip. We've collaborated on a song which they've just recorded. I'm continually stimulated by their appetite for living. Every moment is endowed with great value. Everything they do, from making music to preparing a meal, is touched with love of beauty.

No matter how close we've grown, there are moments when I draw myself back to realize how special they are and how privileged I am to know them. It's quite possible that they're too good to be true!

SONNY JURGENSEN

TV sportscaster/former professional
football quarterback

PAT RICHTER

Lawyer/former professional football
tight end

Jurgensen: For seven seasons we roomed together during training camp and on the road. Our room was called Le Club. It was the biggest room in training camp where everyone would come in to unwind and where we would drink tang and vodka or order thirty chilidogs at four in the morning. It was like an all-night café.

I don't know if they put us together for me to try to break him down and make him looser or for him to try and straighten me out. But I was hoping some of Pat's off-the-field intellect would rub off on me.

Pat was so straight. He was the guy who always stayed in the room. He always had to call me in the middle of the night at some bar to tell me that they had caught me during bed check. Then I'd get back to training camp because the fine was like a meter running at a hundred dollars an hour.

Being my roommate and being a tight end, I had to promise to throw to him a lot. And when Pat's family came to the game, instead of throwing it right to him, I threw the ball a little out of his reach so he could make the spectacular catch.

Richter: We complement each other. We're comfortable with each other. I respect him. Hell, if he were a gal, we'd probably get married.

BEATRICE SYPHAX EVERSLEY
Teacher

FRED EVERSLEY
Sculptor

Beatrice: He is the best gift I ever got. I always thought he was pretty wonderful, and I always told him. When he was a little kid, I used to go around patting his chest saying, "You're wonderful. You're wonderful." Later I'd see him playing in the house, and he would be patting his chest saying, "I'm wonderful." I always wondered whether subliminally that made a difference.

I enjoyed Fred, and he knew it. I still enjoy being with him. As my friends tell me, I smile a lot when I'm with him. I think he's pretty great, and if your mother thinks you're great, you'll make it no matter what anybody else thinks.

SCOTT HORTEN
Student, special education school

ROLAND STURGIS
Student, special education school

Scott: He wheels me and pushes me. He plays ball with me. He makes me laugh. He eats with me.

His hair, eyes, nose, mouth is different and his legs are different. He can walk. He's teaching me to walk.

Roland: He can't walk, and he trying to. When he try to walk, he walk kind of crooked, but I don't make fun of him. That is not nice. That is very rude.

I like him very much. I like to teach him things. I like to teach him to play catch, play basketball. I hope he grow up so he could be basketball player.

CHARLIE WESMER
Sales

SUZIE GOOKIN
Journalist

Wesmer: She entertains me; she's a lot
more fun than anybody I know. Instead of
me being on all the time, I can relax and
turn myself off for awhile.

We're both very interested in finding somebody. It's not happening, but we keep trying anyway. We talk about how we're going
ing about it. We know we're doing it the
wrong way by going to parties and clubs.

We talk about that stuff, but she doesn't
know any more than I do. I wouldn't like
her if she thought she knew more, because
she'd be preaching to me all the time.

I'm lonely. I don't think people were meant
to be alone, but it doesn't seem nearly as
drastic when you know someone in the
same situation as yourself.

Gookin: When people want to play they
call me. People get old and serious when
they stop playing. Charlie has joi de vivre.

She worries about me because she thinks
I don't know how to work or make money.
She knows how. She wants me to get a
job and not just go to parties and starve
genteelly. She's like a little mother hen.

I don't want other people to know I'm
helpless 'cause I have this big act. She has
it all together, and she's going to help
me get my cupboard pristine and my
financial systems in order. Then I'll be
all together—like the modern American
woman!

MARGIE SEIDES
Homemaker/dance therapist

MINDY WEISEL
Homemaker/artist

Weisel: When I moved next door, she ran
out and put her arms around me and said,
"I'm so happy to see someone who looks
like you!" We've fed off each other since
then, feeding each other's desires to be
more than we were—mothers with three-
year-old daughters.

She and I share a secret world that no one
else knows about. We allow ourselves to
live out our fantasies. I tell her my fantasy,
and she'll take it seriously and often not
know whether I lived it out or not. But I
know she really knows.

She takes care of needs that are very old,
like when I'm feeling particularly down,
she'll bring me napoleons in bed like my
mother used to do when I was a child. She
allows herself to play the past for me in
the present.

We collaborate on life. We're each other's
music. We spark off each other in everything—dance, painting, mothering, husbands, lovers. Lovers are the fantasy thing.

Seides: Most of my friends are locked into
the surburban thing. They're not doing
other things. They don't understand the
need I have to dance, to work, to spend
time out of my house.

There's no way I can just be a mother or
a wife. I have to have something I can call
mine, just mine. I want to make it all work,
and it doesn't always work. Mindy under-
stands.

BILLIE DAVIDSON
Private detective

PHILIP DAVIDSON
Private detective

Philip: She works for me not because she's my daughter, but because she's smart and enthusiastic and has the right instincts for this kind of business.

San Juan was a textbook case where Billie was perfect. We were looking for these two guys. We arrived at six on a Sunday morning and went right to the hotel. We were sitting in the lobby, waiting. I was bushed—I'm no spring chicken anymore—and began to doze.

She went out to the pool and spotted them going to the elevator. She picked their description just like that. She's good on ID. I don't think I'm any better or maybe as good on ID. It took me years to get there. She picked it up right away.

Billie: I pulled my hat down real low and got on the elevator with them. I was waiting for them to push the button to see what floor they were going to. They hit eight, and then I hit nine. So I knew what floor they were on.

On the elevator they're chitchatting and calling each other by name, so I was sure I had the right guys. And I hear them tell their girlfriends to be ready by one o'clock so they could go to the casino. So I knew what time they were leaving. I got off the elevator and frantically ran back downstairs to tell the Old Man. It was beautiful, a classic.

The Old Man taught me real good, God love him, and he was pleased.

NORMA STORCH
Writer

LARRY STORCH
Comedian

DIGBY
Cat

Larry: Digby's my constant companion.
I'm never lonesome. He's family. He's the
child we never had.

Norma: He gives me absolute love. I can
be bitchy and tired, and Digby will still
keep giving me the same love and affection.
He's patient and will wait until I'm ready
to receive him.

He's just such a little gentleman, an aristo-
crat, and we are his slaves.

MERCEDES EICHHOLZ

CAROLYN AGGER FORTAS
Lawyer

Eichholz: It's been so long that I don't remember why we became friends. But I remember when I first met her. I was a magnolia blossom right out of Louisiana when I came to Washington. We were taken to their house and introduced.

Here was this very smart lady lawyer with bobbed hair and high heels. I was floored by her. I had never seen anybody like her in my life. We started seeing each other because our husbands worked together, and we just became very fond of each other.

When I'm down or things are rough going, I can always count on Carol to bolster me. If I screamed to Carol and said, "Help, I can't stand it another minute," she'd come and shake me and put sense in my head, and see that I was all right.

Fortas: She was a young married woman when I first knew her. We both liked to dance and go to parties. That started our friendship. Since I am eight years older than she is, she seemed very young to me at that point; the distance of eight years isn't as great as it was then. In some ways I supported her originally through more experience, and since she was much more practical than I was, she supplemented my lack of practicality.

I can talk to and depend on her. She gets after me to do things, which I need. She gives me good advice, sought and unsought.

ANDY WONG
Caretaker

JOSEPH HIRSHHORN
Art collector/philanthropist

Hirshhorn: He looks after me like I was his father or brother. There's feeling about it. He really likes me.

One night I had gone to sleep feeling pretty bad. At two o'clock in the morning, my bedroom door opens. It's Andy, and he's shining a flashlight in my face. He wanted to see how I was. He was worried about me. He did that two or three times that night. I appreciate that.

He's a good boy. I'm nice to him too. I don't impose on him. I don't say "Get me this," I say "Andy, please get me this." I don't boss people around, only my wife.

Wong: When a person speaks to him, you feel to keep down your face a little lower. It don't mean he's too short. It means respect, like a pupil speak to a teacher.

He's so powerful and successful man. He's got sharp eyes and intelligent and a hard-working man. He has a lot of joy. He's a good master and a good teacher.